Library of Congress Facsimile No. 1a

"There is but one entrance by sea into this country, and that is at the mouth of a very goodly Bay…Within is a country that may have the prerogative over the most pleasant places of Europe, Asia, Africa, or America, for large and pleasant navigable rivers: heaven and earth have never agreed better to frame a place for man's habitation…."
>   Captain John Smith, *Description of Virginia*, 1612

THE DISCOVERY OF THE CHESAPEAKE BAY

An Account of the Explorations
of Captain John Smith
in the Year 1608

By: FRANCIS d'A. COLLINGS

With illustrations by: LEONARD VOSBURGH

Chesapeake Bay Maritime Museum
1988

Editorial director: Richard J. S. Dodds
Editor: Beverly Grace Abribat
Designer: Leonard Vosburgh

Library of Congress Cataloging-in-Publication Data

Collings, Francis d'A., 1929-
    The discovery of the Chesapeake Bay: an account of the explorations of Captain John Smith in the year 1608; with illustrations by Leonard Vosburgh.

    Bibliography: p.
    1. Chesapeake Bay Region (Md. and Va.)—Discovery and exploration. 2. Indians of North America—Chesapeake Bay Region (Md. and Va.)—History. 3. America—Discovery and exploration—English. 4. Smith, John, 1580-1631—Journeys—Chesapeake Bay Region (Md. and Va.) I. Title
F187.C5C63 1988   910'.0916347--dc19   88-23703 CIP
ISBN 0-922249-00-8

Copyright © 1988 by Francis d'A Collings, in text. Illustrations copyright © 1988 by Chesapeake Bay Maritime Museum. All rights reserved under International and Pan-American Copyright Conventions. No part of this book may be reproduced or utilized in any form or by any means, electronic or mechanical, including photocopyings, recording, or by any information storage and retrieval system, without permission in writing from the publisher. Inquiries should be directed to Chesapeake Bay Maritime Museum, Navy Point, P. O. Box 636, St. Michaels, Md. 21663.
Printed and bound in the United States of America.

THE DISCOVERY OF THE CHESAPEAKE BAY
TABLE OF CONTENTS

    page

Preface i

1. Where No Christian Knowne Ever Was 1

2. The Lower Eastern Shore 7

3. These Unknowne Large Waters 14

4. The Potomac River 18
       English Ship's Boat (illus.)..............................26

5. The Scumme of the World 28
       First Expedition (map) 33
       Second Expedition (map) 34

6. The Massawomecks 35

7. The Susquehannocks 40

8. The Righte Course How to Proceede 44

9. The Memory of Time 51

   A Note on Sources 57

   Appendix (Crew Lists) 59

   Smith's 1612 Map of Virginia ....inside covers

Preface

Captain John Smith (1580–1631) was the first European to explore the Chesapeake Bay. During the summer of 1608, he and a handful of men from the year-old English settlement at Jamestown took a small open boat on two extensive trips up the Bay, eventually reaching its head where it merges into the Susquehanna River. They experienced formidable dangers and hardships on the way, including numerous encounters with hostile Indians, yet returned safely and in good spirits with the loss of only one man, who died of natural causes.

Others would follow later and map in the details, but it was Smith's little expedition which first established the shape and extent of this, the largest estuary in North America, and proved conclusively that it was not the hoped-for passage through to the Western Ocean. Four years later, back in England, he would draw up a map of the Bay which can still be used as a guide today without going too far astray.

Much has been written, both at that time and later, about Captain Smith's role in the founding of Jamestown, which was the first English settlement on the continent to survive, predating that of the Pilgrims at Plymouth, Massachussetts, by more than a dozen years. The Captain has also become well known to generations of American schoolchildren for his supposed romantic relationship with the Indian princess Pocahontas — a fame which, could he have known of it, would probably have astonished him, since he never gave much importance to matters of the heart, and throughout his life paid little attention to women except when he needed their help.

But there is very little literature available on his discovery of the Bay, which in most histories is treated as a diversion. This is curious, because it was perhaps the most unqualified achievement in the career of this difficult and contentious man — the adventure of which, on looking back, he would have been most proud.

This account therefore aims to fill a small gap in the historical record and, at the same time, provide instruction and entertainment to those who know and love the Bay today. It is the fruit of several summers under sail spent retracing, bit by bit, the path of the explorers, with interludes of more sedentary research into the surviving accounts of the time, including those written by Smith himself. Sailing and history can be nicely complementary hobbies. After all, cruising with a purpose is more fun; and what better way is there to imagine what it was like during that faraway summer when America was new, than to place oneself as nearly as possible in the way of similar experiences today?

Like many of the other English adventurers brought up in the age of Elizabeth I, Smith was not only a man of action but also, despite his cursory formal education, extremely literate and imbued with a strong sense of history. He shaped events with his pen as well as with his sword. But the recognition and acclaim he so vigorously sought largely eluded him during his lifetime. When he died, at an advanced age by the standards of his time, he was poor, alone and unmourned.

The story of the discovery of the Chesapeake Bay shows the oft-maligned Captain Smith at his best. I like to think that his ego, which must have become very bruised in later life, would be flattered if he could know that someone in the impossibly distant future would take the trouble to go where he went, read what he said about it, and tell the story over again.

In the Captain's own words, I wish the reader "...a flowne sheet, a faire wind, and a buone voyage."

F.d'A.C. Washington D.C.
January 1988

1. Where No Christian Knowne Ever Was

"Cape Henry, on the south side of the entrance, has a prominent range of sand hills about 80 feet high…Cape Henry light, 164 feet above the water, is shown from a 163-foot octagonal, pyramidal tower, upper and lower half of each face alternately black and white, on the beach near the turn of the cape…."

U.S. Coast Pilot 3, Atlantic Coast, 1983.

"The cape on the south side is called Cape Henry in honour of our most noble Prince. The shew of the land there, is a white hilly sand like unto the Downes, and along the shore great plentie of Pines and Firres."

John Smith, Description of Virginia, 1612.

ₔ ₔ ₔ

Cape Henry has never been anything very remarkable to see. From the sea, you will now see some low sandhills scattered with hotels and summer cottages, and two lighthouses (one, the abandoned 1791 original), behind a barely perceptible curve in the beach. But this place has been important in America's history. It is the traditional point of landfall or departure for ships entering and leaving the Chesapeake Bay — the body of water around whose shores the first permanent settlement of what is now the United States began.

A few cable lengths off this spot, on the fine morning of June 2, 1608, the Virginia Company of London's ship *Phenix* (Captain Martin), which had just come downriver from the new English colony at Jamestown, hove to briefly. A heavily-laden boat being towed astern was brought alongside, and into it clambered 15 men. As they were cast off, there were no doubt some cheers and a bit of ribald banter about the girls they all hoped to encounter soon. Then the *Phenix* hauled in her sheets and got underway again, homeward bound for England. The men left behind in the boat unshipped oars and began rowing towards Cape Charles at the opposite side of the Bay entrance, hazily visible on the northern horizon. Within an hour the two vessels were out of sight of each other and the seascape returned to its normal timeless emptiness.

The *Phenix* made a quick passage back to London, which was probably lucky, since she had the reputation of being a phenomenally unweatherly ship. On the outward voyage some months earlier she became separated from the *Susan Constant* (Captain Newport), with which she was in company, and actually sighted Cape Henry before being driven out to sea again by contrary winds. She eventually wound up all the way down in the West Indies where Captain Martin, making the best of things, pillaged a few Spanish outposts before returning for a second attempt, this time successful, to enter the Chesapeake Bay.

This story, however, concerns not the *Phenix* but rather the boat she left behind. In its sternsheets sat the small upright figure of Captain John Smith, then a Councilman of the Jamestown settlement and soon to become its President. Of the others in the boat, six are identified as "gentlemen," which probably meant to the class-conscious settlers that they did not expect to do much rowing. One, Walter Russel, was a "doctour of physicke." Among those of a humbler sort was an enigmatic young man named Anas Todkill who served as a personal henchman of the Captain and, having some education, collaborated with Dr. Russel to write the only surviving log of their trip.

The boat they were in is described only as "...an open barge of two tunnes burthen." It had no name: when necessary, they referred to it as "the discovery barge." It was probably built in England and towed across, or carried in pieces. It would have been the typical ship's boat of the time: about 30 feet in length, broad and heavy, designed primarily to be rowed but also carrying two masts with a loose-footed lugsail on each. Its performance under sail would have been dismal compared to any modern yacht, but at least the men could rest their oars when there was a favorable wind. To the Indians, as will be seen later, it represented high technology.

By this time the area around the James and York Rivers near Jamestown had been fairly thoroughly explored, but no one knew where the main Bay itself, which extended an unknown distance to the north, might lead. Some believed that it would provide passage through to the great Western Ocean which obliging Indians told them lay just beyond the mountains to the west (they could have been referring to the Great Lakes or the Gulf of Mexico, but more likely they simply invented this ocean to please the visitors). Others in the boat were more interested in the prospect of finding gold and silver mines which were rumored to be in the area. A third aim of the expedition was to look for traces of the lost colonists who had disappeared mysteriously from Sir Walter Raleigh's settlement at Roanoke (North Carolina) two decades earlier, and, it was thought, might have found refuge somewhere up the Bay.

Captain Smith himself, while evidently not insensible to the honor and glory that might be his if any of these things were found, seems as much to have been motivated by the sheer joy of exploring unknown places and being the first into this region where he believed (not quite accurately, in fact) "no Christian knowne ever was."

So, what sort of a man was this, of whom the eminent historian John Fiske would write nearly three centuries later: "To this day John Smith is one of the personages about whom writers of history are apt to lose their tempers."?

When today you look at his portrait you may feel a shock of recognition, because you know this man. His type is altogether familiar in modern times: small, bristly, energetic, impatient, ambitious, vain; a leader of men and a mover of events; a perennial achiever who is thrust early into positions of power and responsibility but who somehow just misses greatness, mainly on account of an abrasive personality. The eyes that look out at you are alert and knowing, like those of a highly intelligent rat. He could be charming at one moment, ruthless the next. Others admired or hated him, depending on how he used them, but few seem to have really liked him. He had followers or enemies, but no friends.

His earlier life had been eventful even by the standards of an adventurous time. He was born in Willoughby, Lincolnshire, in 1580, the son of respectable yeomen-class parents. At age 16, he left home for France as companion to one of Lord Willoughby's sons who was embarking upon his "grand tour." Finding this dull, Smith then enlisted as what we would now call a mercenary in the fighting against the Spanish in Flanders. An outbreak of peace bringing this activity to an end, he next signed up with the Duc de Mercoeur (whom he persistently called Duke Mercury) for an expedition against the Turks in Hungary and Transylvania.

His own account of this campaign borders on the incredible, although other evidence does broadly corroborate it. At the siege of Regall in 1602, he claims to have slain and beheaded three Turkish gladiators in a formal combat arranged, apparently, to amuse ladies on both sides who were becoming bored with the military stalemate. This feat earned him the coat of arms with three turbanned heads which decorates his 1612 *Map of Virginia*. But otherwise the campaign did not go well. Hundreds of the Duke's men died in the cold, and eventually Smith himself was captured by the Turks and sold as a slave. As luck would have it, he was brought by a wealthy Sultan who presented him to his young sister as a gift. She, Charatza Tragabandza by name, soon became enamored of Smith and, doubtless with some encouragement from him, developed a plot to raise him to marriageable status by sending him off to visit her brother's camp in an outlying province. By this time the Sultan's eyes must have opened to what was going on, because he promptly had an iron collar riveted around Smith's neck and chained him to a wall. After some time Smith managed to catch the Sultan unawares, kill him, and make his escape. But he never forgot Charatza. Many years later, he would name a headland in New England (now called Cape Ann) after her. This is more than he ever did for Pocahontas.

Following this adventure he found himself back in England without gainful employment. But soon he heard about the recently-formed Virginia Company which, with the backing of King James, was undertaking a new attempt to establish a colony on the eastern seaboard of North America. A natural for this kind of enterprise, he joined up promptly. The settlers, aboard *Susan Constant* and two smaller vessels, left the South Downs astern on New Year's Day, 1607, and reached the Virginia Capes in May after a dreadful voyage via the West Indies. Smith was in chains again on arrival, having been arrested en route for suspected complicity in a mutiny plot, a charge he furiously denied. He had to be released when they landed because, embarrassingly, upon opening a sealed box of instructions from the King, it was discovered that he was appointed as a member of the new colony's governing council.

The story of the first year at Jamestown has been copiously chronicled. It seems that everyone there who could write, including Smith himself, spent much of their time penning separate and often contradictory accounts of all that happened. These events need not concern us here except to note that Smith quickly established himself as a key, if controversial, figure in the colony's affairs. He was able to do this partly because of the conspicuous absence of other natural leaders. He was one of the few to realize that, if they were not all to starve to death during that first terrible winter (when in fact about half of them died), they would have to beg, buy or steal food from the Indians. He set about doing this, which is how he met Pocahontas. But he came to prominence also because the social and political environment of the new colony allowed full scope for his special brand of manipulative talents. The moral tone of the settlers, at this time all male, was nothing like as elevated as that of the Puritans who landed at Plymouth Rock a few years later. Jamestown was a commercial venture, and as such it had attracted a raffish, greedy, quarrelsome bunch of adventurers, ever at loggerheads with each other but at least disposed to recognize authority when they saw it. In these surroundings, a man like Smith rose to the top like a bubble in water; he just could not be kept down.

This, then, was Captain John Smith, in his 28th year, as he took command of 14 other men in a small boat and rowed away from the *Phenix* at Cape Henry on June 2, 1608, "...to performe his discoverie."

Why was there only one boat? One would think that the security of an expedition like this would have been immeasurably improved if there had been at least two traveling together. It is true that the colony was short of boats and men to row them. But another possibility is that there were many among the bickering members of the Council at Jamestown who were prepared to approve the venture only if minimally equipped, in the hope that Smith would never return. In this, they were to be twice disappointed.

2. The Lower Eastern Shore

"The people of these rivers are of little stature, of another language from the rest, and very rude."

John Smith, *Description of Virginia*, 1612.

🐚   🐚   🐚

After separating from the *Phenix,* the trip across the broad waters of the Bay entrance from Cape Henry to Cape Charles would have taken them about three hours. Their course would be parallel to the line of the modern bridge-tunnel which nowadays carries a constant stream of heavy road traffic, serpent-like, over and under the water.

Arriving at the other side, they landed on a small island which the Captain named—what else?—Smith Island. There are two Smith Islands on the modern map of the Bay: one 30 miles further up the Eastern Shore, and the other a short distance up the seaward side of the peninsula, where now stands the 180-foot Cape Charles light tower. The latter is the spot designated by local tradition as the site of Smith's first landing. But this is unlikely. No prudent mariner heading up the

Bay itself would detour by the exposed outer coast and land through the surf on this isolated sandbank. However, there was until comparatively recent times another island off the tip of the present-day Cape. It is shown on Smith's own *Map of Virginia* as being of substantial size. As late as 1860 it appeared on a progress sketch of the U.S. Coast Survey, by that time divided into two islands of a few acres each. Now there is only a shoal of 6-12-foot depth named Nautilus Bank. This was almost certainly the original landing place, now completely washed away.

While looking about this place, they suddenly encountered "...2 grimme and stout salvages...with long poles like Javelings, headed with bone. They boldly demanded what we were and what we would...." The fishermen were probably quite as startled as the explorers by this sudden apparition in their midst. As would happen repeatedly, they were at first truculent and suspicious, but soon became friendly. It turned out that these people were members of the Chesapeake tribe, whose name had already been given to the whole Bay, and unlike the other natives further up, they spoke the Powhatan language of the Western Shore with which Smith and several of his men had become familiar.

After suitable preliminaries, the two men invited the English to visit their King at a place called Ackawamacke (the area is now Accomack County, Virginia). Here they were "kindly intreated." The King they described as "the comliest proper Salvage wee encountered." He was a jolly fellow and a great talker. He told them a long and complicated story about two dead children of his people who had taken to rising from their burial places to haunt the village. He also "...made such descriptions of the Bay, isles and rivers that often did us exceeding pleasure." This may have been his way of encouraging the visitors to move on without too much delay.

Move on they did, proceeding slowly along the lower Eastern Shore looking for possible harbors or human habitations. They found nothing much to interest them for the first 30 or so miles, since the coastline here is mainly beach and swamp with scrubby forest behind. Then they spied some islands out in the Bay and bore up to investigate.

Before reaching the islands the boat was struck by a typical

Chesapeake thunderstorm: "... such an extream gust of wind, raine, thunder and lightening happened, that with great daunger, we escaped the unmercifull raging of that ocean-like water." Exactly such summer storms appear suddenly on the Bay today, and an hour later are gone as if they had never been.

They anchored for the night off one of the islands, probably Tangier. Many such nights must have been spent dozing uncomfortably in a sitting position against the sides of the boat, since there would not have been room for all of them to lie down. But this was considered safer than camping on an unknown shore where ambush and arrows out of nowhere could bring sudden death. The next morning they went ashore and explored the swampy terrain, which nowhere rises more than a foot or so above the tideline. They found no fresh water and no inhabitants, although the place was habitable, they thought (Tangier now supports a population several times larger than that of Jamestown at the time.). They moved on to the next island, now called Smith Island, with similar results. They named the group "Russel's Islands," after the doctor, but this name has not stuck.

Now urgently in need of water, they returned to the eastern mainland, where they came across their first river of any size. This was the Wicomico (not to be confused with two other rivers over on the Western Shore later named Wicomico). A little way up this river they met a new lot of Indians, a small timid group eking out a marginal existence in the salty marshlands. At first they seemed hostile, but this was probably more from fright than anything else. After a few gifts they became "very tractable." The English took ruthless advantage of their hospitality, searching through the mean encampment and digging holes all round in search of water. What they found they described as "...such puddle that never till then wee ever knew the want of good water." But after two days, having found nothing better, they lowered their standards and allowed "...wee would have refused two barricoes of gold for one of that puddle water of Wighcocomico."

In the end they managed to assuage their thirst at a place they called Point Ployer, where they reported finding high ground and "a great pond of fresh water, but so exceeding hot we supposed it some bath." The location of Point Ployer must remain a mystery, since nowhere in this area does the ground rise more than a few feet above the water and the coastline is mostly saltmarsh. Perhaps they were deluded by an edge of the forest coming close to the shore, which in the Bay country often looks like a solid cliff. And perhaps, tormented by thirst and the squadrons of huge mosquitoes which inhabit this region, they were all too willing to imagine some shallow brackish lake into their great pond. In any event, they were refreshed by it, and made ready to move on.

Next they went out to the islands again. What they were looking for here is nowhere stated, but it probably had to do with persistent rumors that the survivors of the Roanoke colony had taken refuge somewhere around here. The early settlers' preference for establishing themselves on small islands, for reasons of defense, would have suggested these Bay islands as a likely place.

They found nothing, of course; and neither they nor anyone since has ever established conclusively what became of the lost colonists. When an English ship returned to Roanoke two years behind schedule to look for them — the intervening time had been that of the Spanish Armada, when every available ship was requisitioned for the defense of England's shores — they found the settlement abandoned and overgrown, with the only sign of what had happened the word "CROATAN" carved on a tree. The Croatans were a friendly tribe located near Cape Hatteras, who had migrated inland by the time the search party arrived. It seems most probable that the colonists were attacked by another, hostile, tribe, and what survivors there were took refuge with the Croatans, who then themselves were forced to flee. Because it was not the Indian habit to spare men defeated in battle, the survivors would have been mostly women and children, who perforce would have been incorporated into the host tribe. Among them would have been the baby girl, Virginia Dare, the first English child to be born in North America, and a valuable piece of property by Indian standards.

As late as the mid-nineteenth century, there was a tribe of Indians in Robertson County, North Carolina, called the Hatteras. These people included an unusual number of fair-haired, blue-eyed types, some with surnames similar to those of the lost colonists. Their language included archaic English words of the Elizabethan period. This is where at least one eminent modern authority, Samuel Eliot Morison, believes the survivors from Roanoke ended up. There is no evidence that any of them ever reached the Chesapeake Bay.

The discoverers' second visit to the islands was as unsatisfactory as the first. Another violent storm almost sank them, blowing the foremast over and ripping the sail which they had to patch with their shirts. Bad weather persisted for two days, during which they were forced to huddle ashore, probably on Bloodsworth Island, a featureless swamp now used by aircraft from the U.S. Naval Air Station at Patuxent for bombing practice. This miserable place they named, appropriately, "Limbo."

Their zigzag course up what is now called Tangier Sound took them back to the mainland again, and a large navigable river they called Kuskarawaock or Kuskaranoek. This was undoubtedly the Nanticoke River, which carries three or four fathoms for more than 30 miles inland. And here they had their first really threatening confrontation with the native people, one which could easily have ended the whole endeavor before it had barely begun.

As they rowed up this river, they gradually became aware of many near-naked savages flitting silently from tree to tree along the banks. When nightfall obliged them to anchor in midstream, a few arrows flew from the trees. After an anxious but uneventful night, the sun rose again to reveal on the shore several hundred painted braves dancing, gesticulating, and waving their baskets (shields). They kept up this menacing behavior most of the day, undeterred by the occasional discharge of muskets from the English boat.

Toward evening, the Captain decided to break the deadlock and go in. As the boat approached shore he ordered his men to fire into some reeds where the enemy seemed to be hiding. On landing, it was found that the people had fled, leaving behind "...a many of baskets and much bloud." Inconclusively, Smith retreated to mid-river for another worrisome night at anchor.

Next morning occurred one of those events that restores one's faith in human nature. Paddling upriver came a canoe with four natives who had been out fishing on the Bay and knew nothing of what was going on. They stopped by the English boat for a friendly chat with these curious strangers. Apprised of the situation, they paddled off shorewards to talk things over with their people. Soon there were "...2. or 3. thousand...[surely an exaggeration, but anyhow a large number]...come with gifts." Inexplicably, this chance encounter had triggered a mood-shift from murderous hostility to total friendliness. The Indians seemed to have no in-between. What might have been the end for the English party—an end which would have remained as unknown to the rest of the world as that of the lost colonists—turned into a jolly celebration.

What, one may ask, did the native overlords of the land really think of this puny incursion into their ancestral territory? The hidden eyes which watched the explorer's every move from the river banks would have seen a strange apparition indeed, like an ungainly water beetle with its legs dipping and flashing in the sunlight. The crew were outlandishly dressed in woolen clothes and stovepipe hats: Captain Smith and some of the gentlemen even wore armored metal breast-plates on occasion. The sounds of wood creaking on leather, and harsh foreign voices, would carry far across the water.

The Indians apparently had no premonition that they were witnessing the beginning of the end of their way of life. All the evidence suggests that, at this early stage, they treated the English in the same way that they would have an unfamiliar tribe of their own race—that is, with suspicion and mistrust, but a willingness to extend welcome if honorable excuse were offered. The unpredictable treachery which the discoverers regarded as characteristic of the savages was in fact no more than the way they treated each other. In other words, in 1608 the Red man was prepared to treat the White man as someone not very different from himself.

The English looked on the savages quite differently. Smith found them "...inconsistent in everie thing...craftie, timorous, quicke of apprehension and very ingenious...they are soone moved to anger and so malitious that they seldom forget an injurie...." Their bizarre accoutrements were taken as signs of subhumanity rather than adaptation to circumstances—for example, the clothing of animal skins, the hair worn close-cropped on the right side (to facilitate use of the bow without a self-inflicted scalping), and the dangling decorations of dead rats and dried hands of enemies worn around the belt. One brave carried a live green snake through a hole in his earlobe "...which crawling and lapping herselfe bout his neck often times would familiarly kiss his lips." Smith noted: "Their women are alwaies covered about their midles with a skin and very shamefast to be seen bare."

No Englishman could long forget the appalling cruelty of the Indians towards their captives, in which position they were all too conscious they might find themselves at any time. Smith describes in graphic detail the fate of poor George Curran, a humble Jamestowner abducted the previous winter, who had been skinned alive with mussel shells before being roasted to death over a fire.

Official Virginia Company policy, as formulated back in London, was to avoid violence towards the "naturals" if at all possible. Smith and others on the spot had little patience with the soft approach. He soon developed a normal practice, on first encounter, "to demand their bowes and arrowes, swords, mantles of furres, with some child for hostage: whereby he could quickly perceive if they intended any villanie." If this did not work, a demonstration of English musket firepower could usually be counted upon to produce an appropriate degree of respect without hurting anybody. But, as illustrated on the Nanticoke, he did not hesitate to shoot in earnest if he thought this necessary.

The now-friendly small, rude people of the Nanticoke told Smith that they lived in constant fear of raids from a giant-like race of warriors called the Massawomecks who came from somewhere on the other side of the Bay. He decided that it was time to leave the lower Eastern Shore, which in any event had become "shallow broken isles, and the maine for the most part without fresh water," and go in search of these mysterious beings.

Taking their departure, they headed out through what they called the Straits of Limbo (probably Hooper Strait, the main deep water passage out to the open Bay) and steered north-northwest for the "great high Cliffes" they could faintly discern on the opposite shore.

3. These Unknowne Large Waters

"Maryland is a province situated on the large extending bowels of America."

> George Alsop, (in a tract advertising the advantages of settlement in Maryland), 1666.

ࢶ   ࢶ   ࢶ

The cliffs they eventually came to were the Calvert Cliffs, which stretch up the Western Shore for 20 miles to the north of the Patuxent River mouth. The crossing of the Bay had unwittingly carried the explorers past the entrance to this river, and also to that of the Bay's largest tributary, the Potomac River, which they would not discover until later.

Although there was no sign of human life, they cautiously anchored some distance off the beach for the night. Going ashore next morning, they found a countryside quite different from the waterlogged eastern shore: "…the coast well watered, the mountains very barren, the valleys very fertil, but the woods extream thick, full of Wolves, Beares, Deare, and other wild beasts." Here, although they failed to notice it, can be found reminders of a much more ancient time — fossilized bones and sharks teeth embedded in the soft cliff face. Had they been able to visit the place today, they would have seen some very puzzling sights indeed: offshore, a half-mile-long concrete island on stilts which is used for unloading liquified natural gas from Algeria, and further up the coast the otherworldly towers of the Calvert Cliffs Nuclear Power Station. As it was, they met nobody and saw nothing much to interest them, so they re-embarked in the faithful barge and set off northwards once again.

By this time it must have been abundantly clear to Smith that this could not be the hoped-for strait leading to the Western Ocean. The Bay at this point narrows down to three or four miles in width — a constriction which, in line with Alsop's unfortunate analogy, might be likened to the anus of America. Here the salinity of the water decreases noticeably. Undeterred, however, he pressed on into what is now Maryland (to them it was all part of Virginia) to see what else might be found.

The chronicle written by Russel and Todkill says that they now proceeded for 30 leagues up the western side of the Bay without finding any inlets. A league was three nautical miles, so this meant a passage of about 90 nautical miles. Eventually they came to a river which they named Bolus, after the kind of muddy clay found there, which they thought resembled European bole-armaniac. This is usually taken to be the Patapsco, at the head of which is now the modern port of Baltimore. The distance is about right, but there are other reasons for doubting that they got this far. Even sailing fast before a strong southwesterly wind (which they might well have had at this time of year) it would have taken them more than the one day allotted in the chronicle to make this much northing. Furthermore, they must have been unusually unobservant that day if they sailed right past four substantial rivers (the West, South, Severn, and Magothy Rivers) without even noticing them. Finally, the gluey black mud they report is common in most of the Upper Bay creeks and certainly not unique to the Patapsco. It seem likely that here, as elsewhere during the journey, they exaggerated the distance they had covered. The place where they stopped was probably on the South or the Severn Rivers, in any event, somewhere short of the next major constriction in the Bay now spanned by the twin Bay bridges.

At this point the Captain suddenly had to deal with a near-mutiny. Several of the crew, particularly among the so-called gentlemen, had not bargained for this endless rowing under a hot sun, finding nothing of value and getting ever farther from the relative security of their home base at Jamestown. They were "...oft tired at their oares, their bread spoiled with wet, so much that it was rotten." (The writer, evidently Dr. Russel at this point, adds clinically "...yet so good were their stomacks that they could digest it.") They were probably suffering from exhaustion, dehydration, and exposure. At least half had arrived in North America only a month or two before with the so-called first supply (in either the *Susan Constant* or the *Phenix*), and were not yet seasoned to the ferocious heat of the midsummer Bay.

These men now declared that they would go no further. So Smith stood them on an unknown shore and delivered an oration which is reported in the chronicle as follows:

> Gentlemen, if you would remember the memorable historie of Sir Ralfe Lane, how his company importuned him to proceed in the discoverie of Morattico, alleaging they had yet a dog, that being boyled with Saxafras leaves, would richly feed them in their returnes: what shame it would be for you (that have beene so suspitious of my tendernesse) to force me to return with a month's provision, scarce able to say where we have bin, nor yet heard of that which wee were sent to seeke. You cannot say but I have shared with you the worst that is past; as for what is to come, of lodging, diet, or whatsoever, I am contented that you will allot the worst part to my selfe. As for your feares that I will lose myselfe in these unknown large waters, or be swallowed up in some stormie gust, abandon these childish feares, for worse than is past cannot happen, and there is as much danger to returne as to proceed forward. Regaine therefore your old spirits, for return I will not (if God assist me) til I have seen the Massawomeckes, found Patawomek, or the head of this greate water you conceit to be endlesse.

It seems they all knew the story of Sir Ralph. He was Governor of the first settlement at Roanoke which had to be abandoned and the survivors shipped home in 1586. The incident referred to in Smith's speech occurred during an exploration to the north led by Sir Ralph which may have reached the Bay entrance. The dog they ate, flavored with sassafras leaves, was apparently a stray found in an abandoned Indian village, and not an English dog.

Smith's masterful rebuke got the men back in the boat and headed northwards again. But, unusually, his luck seems to have run out at this point. A strong northerly wind sprang up, which in this shallow and confined part of the Bay quickly whips up a nasty, steep chop against which small boats even with modern engines find it difficult to make headway. Also, it became apparent that several of the men were not malingering; they really were too ill to row the boat.

Captain Smith may have been a man of determination but he was not one to persist against insuperable odds. He finally yielded to the inevitable and turned the boat around to run before the wind. When one does this in a small vessel, the sudden peace that breaks out on board is almost uncanny: one wonders how it can possibly have been so uncomfortable only a moment or so before. It is not difficult to imagine the mixture of feelings — chagrin and relief, frustration and satisfaction — among the men on the boat as, some two weeks after her separation from the *Phenix*, the discovery barge was at last sailing easy and headed back towards more familiar territory.

A day later, while still running south, they unexpectedly came across one of the main things they had been looking for: the mouth of the Potomac. Until then, they had thought it to be still further north of their turning point. But here it was, just a few miles below the place under Richard's Cliffs where they had stopped on the way up, a great river leading westwards into the interior, its mouth so wide that the other side could scarcely be seen.

The condition of the company seems to have improved wonderfully by this time. They now found themselves "...all contente to take some pains to know the name of this 9-mile broad river." John Smith, his luck back in its normal good working order, turned the boat around Point Lookout and headed up to explore a new river.

4. The Potomac River

"The fourth river is called Patawomeke...It is navigable 140 miles, and fed as the rest with many sweet rivers and springs, which fall from the bordering hills."

John Smith, Description of Virginia, 1612

The exploration of the Potomac, from its mouth to the head of navigation some 100 miles up and back (Smith's 140 miles is one of his habitual overestimations), took them somewhere between three and four weeks. That they took so long over this phase of their discovery was partly because they believed it was here they would find the Indian's source of gold and silver. It was not for lack of trying that they failed to locate it.

For the first 25 miles or so they sailed peacefully up the broad river without seeing anyone. Then two Indians in a canoe came out and invited them over to a creek on the south bank which they called Onawmament, probably what is now the Nomini River.

THE POTOMAC RIVER

On entering this creek it was suddenly apparent that an ambush had been prepared. Several hundred savages materialized from the bordering trees "...so strangely painted, grimed, and disguised, showting, yelling and crying, as we rather supposed them so many divels." They made "many bravadoes," rushing at the party in the boat and drawing back. The situation looked ugly.

Preparing for the worst, the Captain had his men load their muskets and discharge them at the treetops. As loud bangs echoed through the forest, flocks of indignant birds rose squawking into the air. But the fusillade had an even more dramatic effect on the Indian war party. They threw their bows on the ground and, after some moments of panic and confusion, emissaries stepped forward from their ranks clearly intent on making peace. This first encounter, typical of many others to follow during their time on the Potomac, illustrates the nerve-jangling uncertainty that must have accompanied each of the expedition's new ventures ashore.

On this occasion, an exchange of hostages was speedily arranged. One John Watkins, identified on the boat's crew list as a soldier, went off with the Indians to a place a few miles inland where the local chief had his seat. We are not told what happened next in this particular instance, but Smith's general description of how the Indians would receive an important visitor is probably indicative:

> If any great commander arrive at the habitation of a Werowance, they spread a mat as the Turkes do a carpet, for him to sit on. Upon another right opposite they sit themselves. Then doe all with a tunable voice of showting bid him welcome. After this, doe 2. or more of their chiefest men make an oration, testifying their love.
>
> Which they do with such vehemency and so great passions, that they sweate til they drop, and are so out of breath they can scarce speake. So that a man would take them to be exceedingly angry or starke mad.
>
> Such victuall as they have, they spend freely, and at night where his lodging is appointed, they set a woman fresh painted with pocones and oile, to be his bedfellow.

At some stage in this now-friendly pow-wow, the Onawmament chief confided that he had been ordered to attack and kill the English intruders, if they showed up, by no less a person that the Great

Powhatan himself. Powhatan was the supreme leader of a confederacy of loosely-related tribes which extended throughout the tidewater area of Virginia all the way up to the Potomac. Powhatan, the chief added, had been put up to this by malcontents from the Jamestown colony who wished to be rid of Smith forever.

Well, perhaps. But it is more likely that the Great Chief had decided for himself that the time had come to be free of his obligation to his troublesome and inquisitive son-in-law, and saw a convenient accident on the fringes of his territory as the best way to do it. We shall never know. But this surmise, if true, suggests two interesting conclusions about political arts among the Indians. One, they were sufficiently sophisticated for the idea of arranging assassination at a distance through intermediaries to be considered feasible. Two, they were not well enough disciplined to carry through such a plot.

But now a digression is necessary to explain how Captain John Smith came to be the Great Powhatan's son-in-law. The story will be familiar to most American schoolchildren. It happened the previous winter, after Smith was captured by a party of Powhatan's men while on an expedition up the York River to get corn. For several weeks he was paraded from village to village. Finally they brought him to the habitation of Powhatan. He was given a hearty meal and then led before the king. Here he was laid out on the ground with his head between three stones, and the tribe's official executioners made ready to bash out his brains with their clubs.

The ceremony, as re-enacted in countless school plays, is just about to begin when there is a flurry among the spectators and onstage rushes Pocahontas, the 13-year-old favorite daughter of Powhatan. She hurls herself down upon the prostrate Captain and begs for his release. Father looks grave, deliberates for a while, and eventually nods in assent. Whew! A mighty celebration ensues, with our Captain and Princess Pocahontas seated together. As the curtain falls, all have become good friends.

What really happened here? Smith's own writings are not very informative on the incident. In fact, in his first published account of these events (the manuscript of which was being carried back to England by the *Phenix* even as the explorers were on the Potomac),

Pocahontas is not even mentioned. This may be because the publisher used his discretion to delete certain parts as "fit to remain private." Sixteen years later when he published his *Generall Historie*, Smith did acknowledge his rescue by Pocahontas, but in tantalizingly cryptic terms: perhaps by then the Captain-turned-author had discovered the value of suspense when writing a romantic tale.

This ambivalence, together with the fact that no other white man was there to corroborate Smith's account, has led skeptics from that time to this to conclude that he made up the whole story. Not likely. Our Captain may have been guilty of embroidering his adventures from time to time, but this one would have been hard to invent.

However, it seems improbable that the wily old Powhatan was so besotted by his daughter that he allowed himself to be swayed by a sudden infatuation on her part. The truth was that the capture of Smith had presented him with an awkward political dilemma. On the one hand, to satisfy the honor of his braves, he was expected to have their prize executed in the appropriate ceremonial manner. On the other hand, he was at this time anxious to make at least a provisional peace with the English. He was interested in these strangers, and realized that there was much they could teach him. He saw that this might be impossible if he allowed one of their important chiefs to be disposed of as tradition required. The long delay before he had the prisoner brought to him shows that he needed time to ponder this problem.

The solution he came up with made use of a convenient custom of his people. Owing to the braves' appalling record of killing each other off in casual warfare, the population had developed a distinct sex imbalance, with a surplus of girls of marriageable age. So it had become accepted that an eligible young woman had the right to claim any interesting-looking captive as her own, provided she undertook to instruct him in the ways of the tribe and make a good warrior-husband out of him. Geneticists will note that this also provided a useful means of introducing new blood into the isolated and hostile tribal families. It was undoubtedly this facility that Pocahontas availed herself of when she rescued John Smith. But it is most unlikely that she would have done this without parental clearance beforehand. And, given the rank of the captive, not any woman could come forward to claim him

—only a princess would do. So it may be surmised that Smith's whole harrowing ordeal was, unbeknownst to him, a "put-up" job. Father had instructed daughter what to do well before the event.

Pocahontas subsequently did her cheerful best to carry out her part of the bargain. After Smith's release, she was a frequent visitor to the English camp. She helped them obtain food, and at least once gave them warning of impending raids, over which her father seems to have had only loose control. She undoubtedly also reported back to him what was going on with the visitors.

And there can be little doubt that she really did fall for John Smith. Her whole behavior during this period is touchingly reminiscent of a modern teenager with a crush. When he, somewhat embarrassed but very conscious of her value to the colony, treated her brusquely and pleaded other pressing business, she redoubled her efforts to get his attention. On one occasion she shocked some of the settlers (and no doubt delighted others) by cartwheeling down their rude main street. Another time she threw a spectacular surprise party for the Captain and his friends which nearly precipitated a disaster. She invited them to a nearby village, ostensibly to parlay with Powhatan, who actually proved to be far away at the time. While they were waiting "...suddainely amongst the woods, was heard such hydeous noise and shreeking, that the English (five of them) betooke theselves to their armes, and seized on two or three old men by them, supposing Powhatan with all his power come to surprise them." Instead, however, from the shadows emerged some 30 near-naked young women led by Pocahontas, who was wearing "a fayre payre of Bucks hornes on her head." For about an hour the visitors were entertained by dancing of "most excellent ill varietie," meaning, unmistakable lewdness. Finally, the Captain reported: "... all those Nymphes more tormented him than ever, with crowding, pressing and hanging about him, most tediously crying, love you not me? Love you not me?" His account stops abruptly: "This mirth and banquet being ended, with firebrands...they conducted him to his lodging."

Many of the colonists wondered why Captain Smith did not marry her. One of them speculated: "...hee had the Salvages in such subjection, hee would have made himselfe a king by marrying

Pocahontas... if he would, he might have married her, or have done what him listed...." However, the idea of marriage between the races was not considered quite proper by Englishmen in the seventeenth century. On this matter, Smith's upright defenders were quick to state: "...nor was it ever suspected hee had ever such a thought, or more regarded her, or any of them, than in honest reason and discreation he might."

What Smith and his friends never grasped was that, in terms of Indian custom, he had already married Pocahontas. Was the marriage consummated? Perhaps, but that is not the point. The real problem was that Powhatan, her father, was not pleased with Smith's failure to become an obedient brave afterwards. That is why Powhatan would have found it quite reasonable to try and have his ungrateful son-in-law murdered at Onawmament.

Escaping at last from the hospitality of the failed assassin, the discovery party re-embarked and continued up the river. They met with at least ten separate tribes on the Potomac, some of whom reacted initially like the Onawmament, while others were friendly from the start. In *Description of Virginia,* Smith gives a list of these tribes and the number of fighting men they could muster. One is struck by how thinly the area was populated then. According to his figures, the entire male workforce of the Potomac basin below Washington, D.C., was about 760, which might have meant a total population of some 4,000. The area is now home to almost half a million persons.

The narrative written by Russel and Todkill does not give us detailed accounts of these other encounters on the Potomac, which are dismissed rather summarily: "To expresse al our quarrels, treacheries and incounters among these Salvages, I should be too tedious." A pity—we would like to have known more.

Many of the places mentioned in Smith's description and shown on his map can be identified today. Cecawone (variously spelled), about 12 miles up on the southern side, is unmistakably the Coan River. The Patawomeck tribe, for which the river was named, is shown just after the first major northwards bend, where there is now a shallow inlet called Potomac Creek. The tributary Smith calls Quiyough, "the greatest of the least," appears to be Aquia Creek, which trends northwest just as he describes. But he indicates it is a substantial river, not much smaller than the Potomac itself, and claims to have explored it for 15 miles. Today, an inflatable dinghy goes aground after two or three miles. It is likely that this and other waterways he describes have silted up heavily in the intervening 375 years because of deforestation of the surrounding countryside. But one suspects that, here again, he exaggerated their distance a bit.

His claim to having followed the main river up to the first falls, however, can be believed. The description of the stretch between present-day Georgetown, D.C., and Little Falls is unquestionably first-hand: "The river...above this place maketh his passage downe a low pleasant valley overshaddowed in manie places with high rocky mountaines, from whence distill innumerable sweet and pleasant springs." Had they gone a short way further upstream they would have come to the much more spectacular Great Falls, where even in June there is usually an impressive flow of water cascading between near-vertical cliffs. That he does not even mention the larger falls suggests that his report is based on what he saw and not hearsay.

As was their custom, when they reached the highest point on the river they carved a cross on a tree, to show that Englishmen had been there.

It is possible that they were not in fact the first white men to ascend the Potomac. In the shadowy times some 40 years earlier, Spaniards in a ship from Florida had pushed up a great river they named Espiritu Santo, which is generally believed to be the Potomac. Somewhere on its banks, they left behind a mission of eight Jesuits led by one Fra. Segura, who was charged with the task of Christianizing the savages and securing the region for Spain. With them was a native from the Chesapeake area who had somehow found his way down to Florida where he had been baptized Don Luis Velasco by the Fathers. During the first winter Don Luis defected back to his people and the eight Spaniards were slaughtered. This was discovered the next summer when another Spanish ship returned to the spot. In reprisal, eight local Indians were seized and hanged from the ship's yardarm.

The explorers made one major excursion into the interior to inspect a reported silver mine, which turned out to be a worthless heap of antimony. This was a severe disappointment to them. Actually, gold and silver are present in the area in small quantities and were mined until comparatively recent times; but there never was any Eldorado here. Sadly, Smith had to report, "concerning the entrailes of the earth little can be said for certaine."

Their guide on this occasion was an unusual native called Mosco, whom they would encounter again on the second trip up the Bay. He had "a thicke blacke bush beard, and the Salvages seldom have any at all ... we supposed him to be some French mans son." They never discovered who he really was, but he quickly made himself useful to the visitors as intermediary, interpreter, and middleman. Could he have been a descendant of one of the Jesuit Fathers?

They found abundant wildlife along the banks of the great river. Some of the species mentioned—deer, opossum, otter and raccoon (which Smith spells variously as aroughcun, rangrouchcrun, rahoughcun, rarowcun, etc.)—remain plentiful in the area today. Others such as bear, wildcat, and flying squirrel have all but disappeared. They were particularly taken with the beaver, which is described as "...bigge as an ordinary water dogge, but his legges exceeding short...his taile somewhat like the forme of a racket, bare without haire, which to eate the Salvages esteem a great delicate."

The life in the river itself also amazed them. As they were finally leaving the Potomac, they came across "...fish lying so thicke in the water, as for want of nets (our barge being driven among them) we attempted to catch them with a frying pan: but we found it a bad instrument to catch fish with...." The English never were much good at fishing, and many times had to steal from the Indians' skillfully-constructed traps. Nowhere do they mention that present-day scourge of the Bay, the jellyfish, which ruins the swimming from early summer onwards. Presumably there were none then.

Out into the Bay and headed southward again, the Captain could not resist naming one more place after himself. Smith Point is still the name of the promontory on the south side of the Potomac entrance.

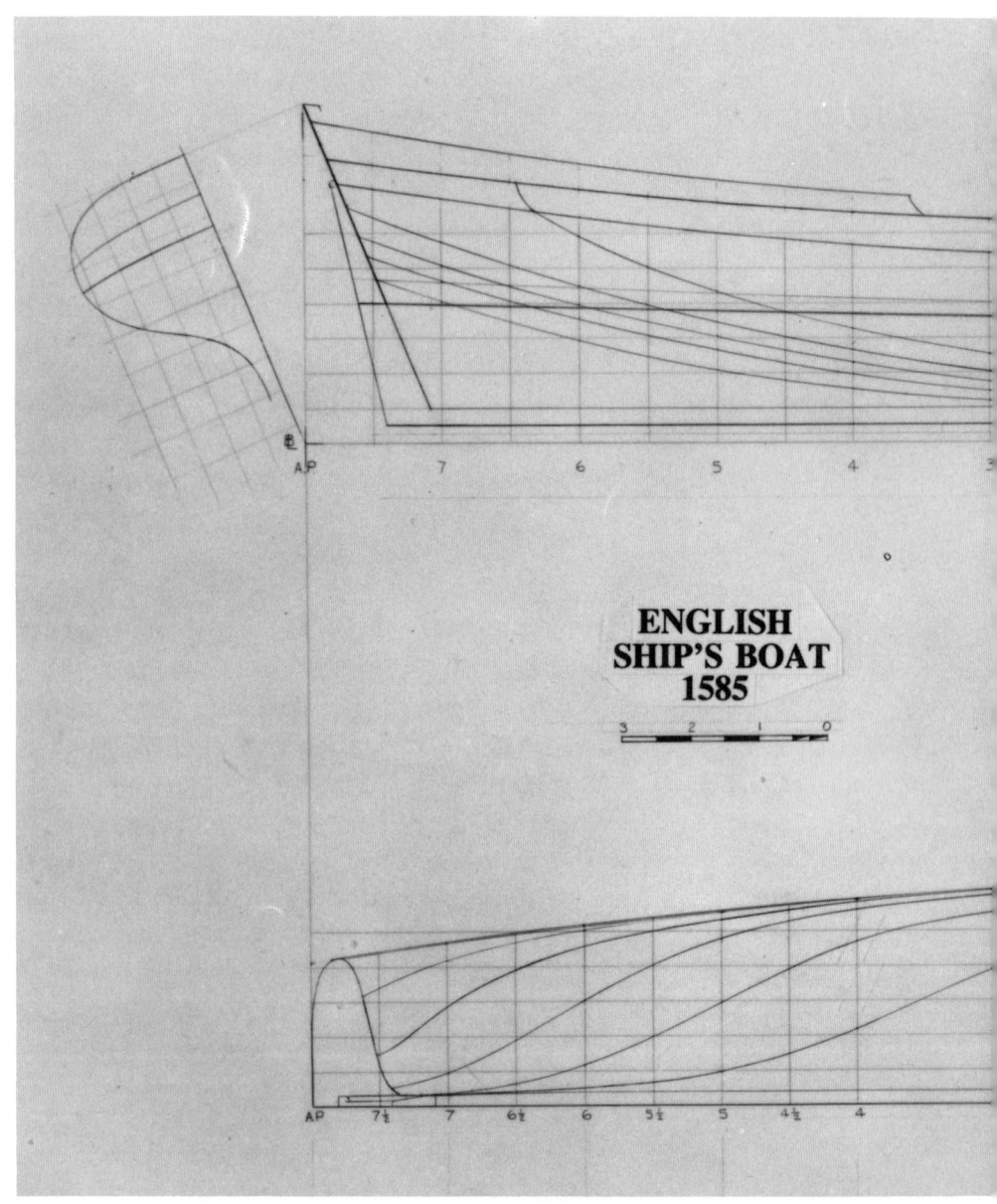

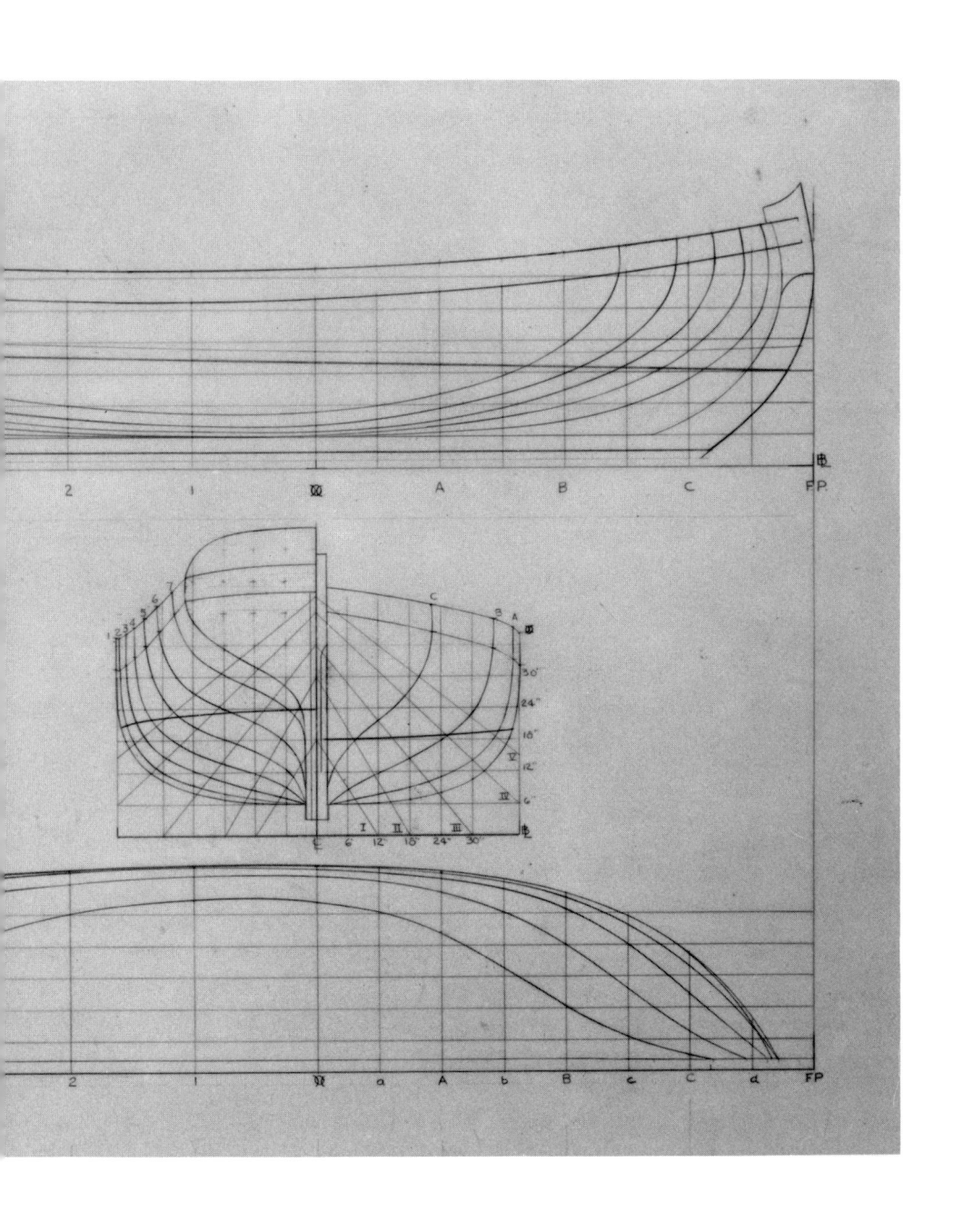

Drawing courtesy of North Carolina Maritime Museum

5. THE SCUMME OF THE WORLD

"For our factions, unless you would have me run away and leave the country, I cannot prevent them...Capitaine Ratcliffe is now called Sicklemore, a poor counterfeited imposture. I have sent you him home, lest the company should cut his throat. What he is now, every one can tell you."

Captain John Smith, in a letter to the
Virginia Company in London, 1608.

ঽ⚓   ঽ⚓   ঽ⚓

After leaving the Potomac, Captain Smith was no less ready than the others to end the exploration and make for home. He was anxious (with good reason, it would transpire) over what had been going on at Jamestown during his long absence. But there was one more river he wanted to investigate en route, the Rappahannock, whose upper reaches he had seen while being held captive by Powhatan's men the previous winter, but whose entrance had yet to be discovered.

They found it only about 20 miles due south of Smith Point. For some reason they entered well over to the southern side, where they ran aground on a sandbank and became firmly stuck. While waiting for the tide to float them off, the explorer and his men hopped overboard and began paddling about in the shallows in search of fish.

What happened next is best told in the words of the chronicle:

> Our Capitaine sporting himselfe to catch them [i.e. the fish] by nailing them to the ground with his sword, set us all a fishing in that manner. By this devise, we tooke in an hour more than we all could eat.
>
> But it chanced, the capitaine taking a fish from his sword (not knowing her condition), being much in the fashion of a thornbacke with a longer taile whereon is a most poysoned sting of 2. or 3. inches long, which shee stroke an inch and halfe into the wrist of his arme.
>
> The which, in 4. houres, had so extreamly swolne his hand, arme, shoulder and part of his body, as we al with much sorrow concluded his funerall, and prepared his grave in an Ile hard by (as himselfe appointed), which we then called Stingray Ile, after the name of the fish.

Stingray Isle does not exist any more, washed away like so many of the Bay's smaller islands by the centuries of erosion; but the place where it was is still called Stingray Point. The fish that stung the Captain was probably of the type *Rhinoptera Bonasus* (cownose ray), which has a venomous barb under its whiplike tail. Descendants of this fish can still be seen on the Bay, basking in shallow water or swimming at a leisurely pace with twin outer fins cutting the surface in such manner as sometimes causes alarmed bathers to report sharks to the Coast Guard.

As nightfall approached, with the grave made ready, the Captain suddenly began to show signs of recovery. Not long after, "his tormenting paine was so wel assuaged that he eate the fish to his supper."

Dr. Russel, who had been applying "precious oile" from his medicine chest to the affected parts, took credit for the cure. But it is more likely that our hero was suffering from an allergic reaction, and it was the robust Smith antibodies that eventually did the trick.

After this incident, Smith, still feeling shaky from the after-effects, was willing to forget about exploring the Rappahanock and run for home. Anyway, the Doctor's supply of precious oil was running out, and no one wanted the patient to have a relapse.

The next day they made the 30-odd miles to Old Point Comfort without difficulty. Rounding into the familiar James River, they stopped for a while at the friendly Indian settlement of Kekoughtan, where several of them had been before. In recent times archaeologists have uncovered relics of this village near the Victorian brick buildings of the Soldier's Home which stands on the east side of the Hampton River. The Kekoughtans, seeing the Captain's arm in a sling and another man injured (apparently he had broken a leg somewhere along the way), assumed that the expedition had been fighting. The unprincipled Smith lost no time in elaborating a story of fierce but victorious action against the dreaded Massawomecks. The locals were much impressed.

Another day carried them most of the way up the river to Jamestown. The mood on that little barge by this time was one of elation. For the final stretch, humorists among the crew used up some remnants of their clothing to decorate it in the fashion of a Spanish pinnace, hoping thus to scare the stay-at-homes into believing that an enemy frigate was following close behind. The record does not describe the reaction of the unhappy people of Jamestown when the identity of this bizarre-looking vessel was finally established.

The day they returned is recorded as July 21, 1608. This meant that they had been gone 49 days. Although their little joke may not have been well received, Captain Smith and his crew were surely entitled to some jubilation over what they had just accomplished. True, they had not found any of the things they were sent to look for. Well aware of this, the restless Smith would be off within a few days to try again. But they had been further up the Bay and its largest river than any White men before them. They had lived off the country in an open boat for seven weeks, survived numerous perils in a strange and barbaric land, and returned in good order without the loss of a single man. This outcome is high tribute to Captain Smith's qualities as a leader. It could easily have been very different.

Without pause Captain Smith plunged into the hornet's nest of Jamestown politics. He found the colony in sorry shape, with most of those who had arrived that spring with the first supply ill of ship's fever (typhus), and the rest "... al unable to do anything but complaine of the pride and unreasonable needlesse cruelty of their sillie President."

They had cause to complain. President Ratcliffe (his real name was Sicklemore, but he had reasons back in England for coming to Virginia under an alias) was a stunningly pompous and dull-witted individual who had allowed the prestige of his office as representative of King James to go to his head. He was no friend of Smith's, and did not forget that Smith had strongly opposed his nomination to the presidency the previous autumn when the first incumbent, President Wingfield, was deposed. Ratcliffe had taken advantage of Smith's absence to appropriate for his own use a large part of the colony's stock of food and supplies. He had also ordered those of the colonists who were not incapacitated to work on a private hunting lodge he was building for himself nearby ("an unnecessarie pallas in the woods," the sarcastic Todkill calls it).

Now, Captain Smith did not have much sympathy for malcontents, whom he later described as "the scumme of the world." He would write scornfully, "...because they found not English cities, nor such faire houses, nor at their own wishes any of their accustomed dainties, with feather beds and downe pillows...[they] had little or no care for any thing but to pamper their bellies, to fly away with our Pinnaces, or to procure their means to return for England." He was referring here to a plot on the part of some of them, which had apparently become common knowledge, to steal one of the boats and sail back to England. Many of the colonists were in truth lazy, scheming, vicious parasites. "Those loyterers...would all have starved, or eaten one another," Smith says elsewhere. Despite his disdain, however, one feels that he understood these weak, frightened, desperate men who by now had realized that death from starvation or Indian attack would be their most likely end. "For the Country was for them," he wrote, "a miserie, a ruine, a death, a hell...."

Smith showed even less patience with the colony's president. Only two or three days after his return, he managed to have Ratcliffe deposed and himself nominated to the presidency. The contemporary accounts of how this was accomplished vary according to which side the writer favored: balanced judgments were rare in the overwrought emotional climate of Jamestown at that time. Smith's supporters blandly explain the Council's choice in terms of "...the good news of our discoverie and the hope we had (by the Salvages relation) our Bay had stretched to the South sea." Despite this outrageous misrepresentation of what the expedition had learned, one can readily imagine that a majority of colonists were deeply relieved to have control over their destiny taken from the incompetent Master Sicklemore alias Ratcliffe and placed in more capable hands.

Actually, the timing of this coup was rather inconvenient for Smith, who longed to get back to the unfinished business of exploration. He immediately deputized one of the recent arrivals, "his deare friend" Matthew Scrivener, to act in his place. No matter that poor Scrivener was at this time "extreamly tormented of a callenture" (fever), and might die any moment. Smith also had various others he trusted appointed to carry on the colony's business and supervise the return of the supplies misappropriated by Ratcliffe.

And this seemed to be about all that he could usefully accomplish in Jamestown for the time being. Those people who were not actually ill were suffering under the full heat of a Chesapeake summer and disinclined to do any productive work. The supply situation was as good as it had ever been, and the Indians seemed peaceful.

So, at this point "...he left them to live at ease and imbarked himselfe to finish his discoverie." There is some confusion over the date on which he set off for the second trip. The first published account says that it was July 20, which is the day before the same account has him returning from the first trip. The date was corrected to July 23 in later accounts, which would be two days after. The second date does not seem much more plausible than the first, since even Smith could hardly have organized a change in government as well as a new expedition into the wilderness in only two days. But clearly the time was short.

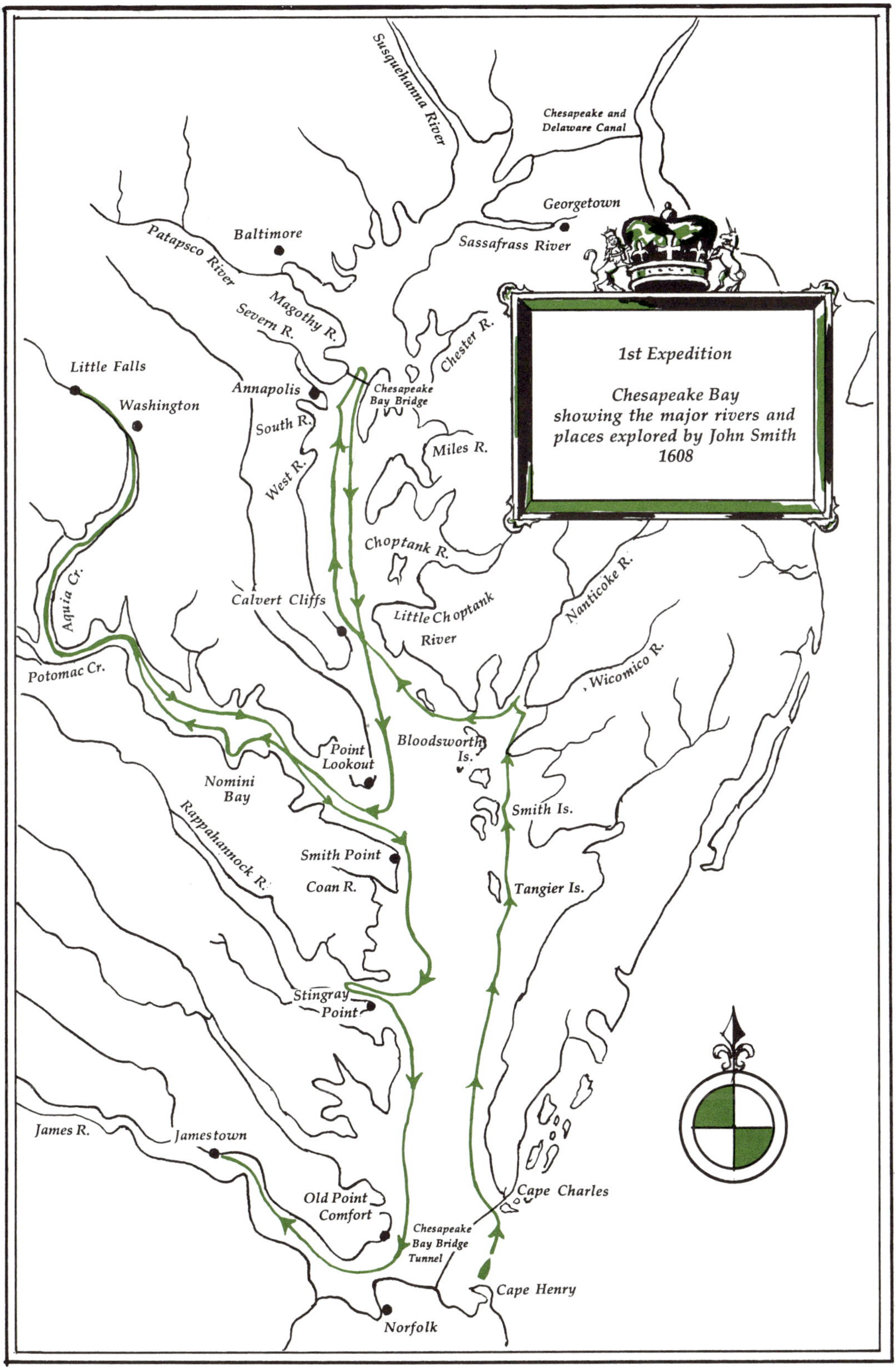
1st Expedition
Chesapeake Bay
showing the major rivers and
places explored by John Smith
1608
Susquehanna River
Chesapeake and
Delaware Canal
Georgetown
Sassafrass River
Baltimore
Patapsco River
Magothy R.
Severn R.
Chester R.
Little Falls
Washington
Annapolis
Chesapeake
Bay Bridge
South R.
Miles R.
West R.
Choptank R.
Aquia Cr.
Calvert Cliffs
Little Choptank
River
Nanticoke R.
Wicomico R.
Potomac Cr.
Bloodsworth
Is.
Point
Lookout
Nomini
Bay
Smith Is.
Rappahannock R.
Smith Point
Coan R.
Tangier Is.
Stingray
Point
James R.
Jamestown
Old Point
Comfort
Cape Charles
Chesapeake
Bay Bridge
Tunnel
Cape Henry
Norfolk

2nd Expedition

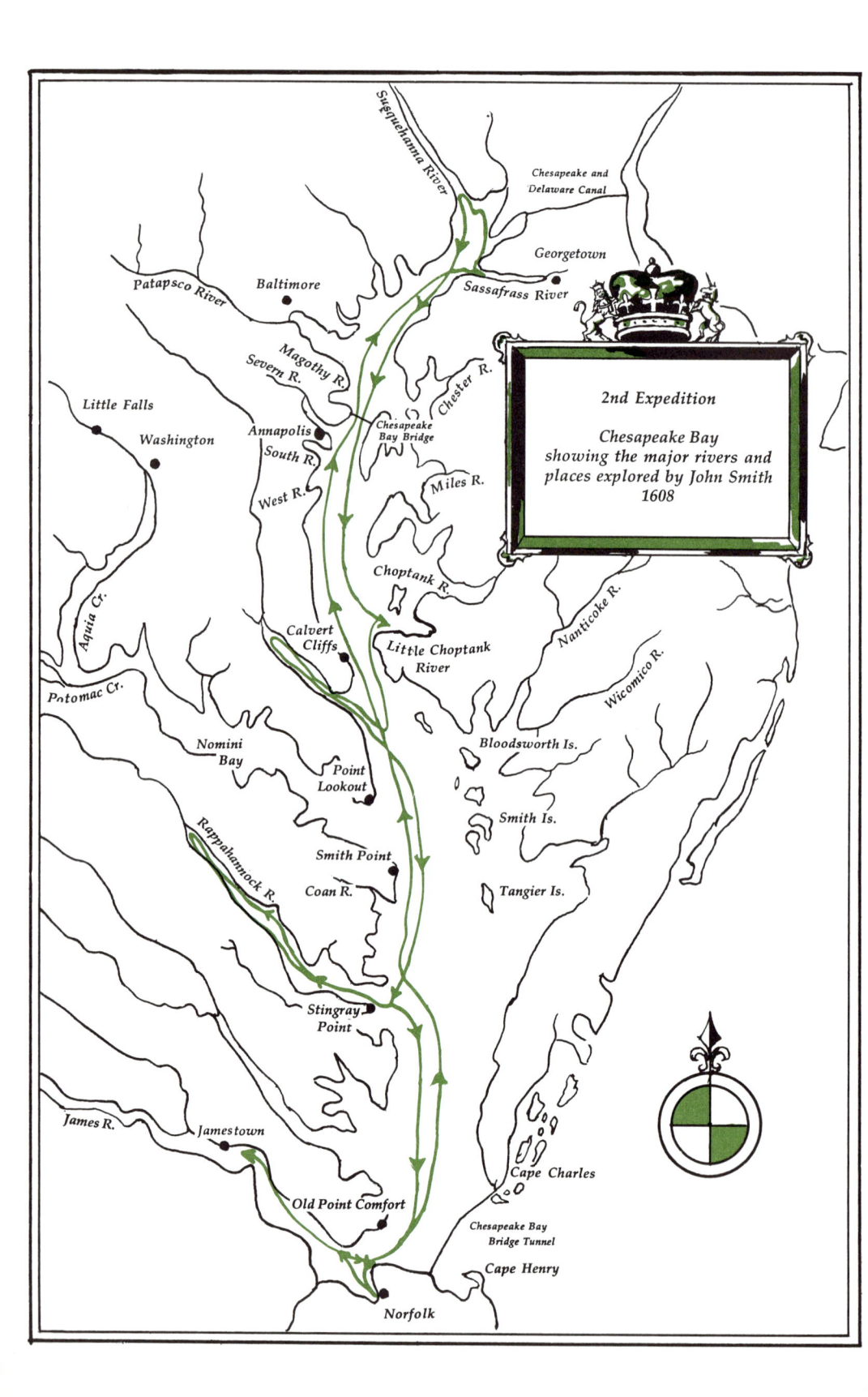

Chesapeake Bay showing the major rivers and places explored by John Smith 1608

6. The Massawomecks

"...so manie men that they made warre with all the world."
                                John Smith, *Generall Historie*, 1624.

ઢ   ઢ   ઢ

The second voyage of discovery was made in the same barge as the first. This time Captain Smith had only 12 men with him. No one seemed to mind that this meant 13 in the boat. Another tribute to his qualities as a leader becomes apparent when one compares the crew lists; no fewer than eight of the 12 who had been on the first trip had volunteered to go again. Among these were Anas Todkill, the chronicler, and John Watkins, the soldier who had gone as hostage with the Indians of the Nomini River. Dr. Russel, who was portly and not young, did not repeat. His place as co-author of the expedition's journal was taken by one Anthony Bagnall, who is listed as a soldier.

Dropping down the James, they called again on their gullible friends, the Kekoughtans of Hampton Creek. Here they were forced by contrary winds to stay over for two or three days. (There seems to have been an unusually high incidence of northerly winds during the summer of 1608.) The Kekoughtans feasted them "with much mirth." These savages were now convinced that the expedition was out to punish the Massawomecks. The English did nothing to disabuse them of this idea: in fact, they returned hospitality by putting on a demonstration of musket fire, to show how they would treat the enemy. This so excited the Kekoughtans that it required all of Smith's diplomatic talents to dissuade them from coming along to join in the fun.

Freeing themselves eventually, they wasted little time in getting up the Bay. They made two long hops, the first back to Stingray Isle (about 40 nautical miles), and the second from there to the place they called Bolus (nearly 90 nautical miles, if it is correct to take this as the Severn River). They must have kept going overnight to have covered these distances non-stop: perhaps there was a moon. As modern voyagers on the Bay quickly discover during July and August, night is often the most comfortable time to make long passages.

After passing the northernmost point of the previous voyage, they came about 30 miles further to a place where the Bay seemingly divides into two branches. This was most likely the mouth of the Patapsco (another indication, by the way, that Bolus cannot have been the site of present-day Baltimore). Another 15 or 20 miles beyond that they noted the Bay dividing into four. This was certainly the confluence of the Sassafras, Elk, Northeast, and Susquehanna Rivers. The freshness of the water would have informed them that they had truly reached the head of the Bay at this point. This is where today ocean-going vessels enter the Chesapeake-Delaware Ship Canal to transit the Delmarva peninsula to the next navigable river system to the north.

They spent some days getting the lay of the land in this confusing area without meeting anyone. They started up the largest river, the Susquehanna, only to find the way barred by rapids after a few miles. Returning, they then sailed off across the Bay to investigate the other side.

While still in open water, they suddenly spied seven or eight big canoes loaded with painted, gesticulating Indians, bristling with weapons, paddling at full speed towards them. Massawomecks! One can imagine that even our steely-nerved Captain felt some fright at this unexpected apparition.

Both sides immediately prepared for hostilities. The English had little to lose from boldness, since at least half of them were so incapacitated as to be barely able to move. They had been like this since shortly after leaving the hospitable Kekoughtans, perhaps as the result of overindulgence in wighsacan, a potent Indian beverage made from fermented roots which, as noted in the *Description of Virginia* "...purgeth ... in a very violent manner." So the Captain had the sick men lie in the bottom of the boat under a tarpaulin, mounted their hats on sticks around the gunwale to give an impression of greater numbers, and held his course.

As the distance between them closed, the terrible Massawomecks suddenly became unnerved and, turning their canoes, fled ignominiously for the shore. Smith followed, sailing silently and inexorably up to where they stood gaping on the beach before dropping anchor a short distance off to await events.

The Indians' alarm may be explained by the fact that they had never seen a boat sailing before. Their own canoes were always propelled by paddles, perhaps because they did not know how to make cloth suitable for sails. The vast gaps between the Indians', Smith's, and our own cultures are nowhere better illustrated than by this incident. To the Massawomecks, the discovery barge embodied seemingly supernatural capabilities: their reaction was like ours might be if an alien interplanetary ship were unexpectedly to land in our midst.

It took some time to lure these timid warriors into a first contact. Eventually two of them braver than the rest set down their arms and came out in one of the canoes. These two were presented with small bells which they took back to show to the others on the shore. Within a few moments, the English boat was surrounded by canoes and people, and a positive orgy of gift-giving got under way. The Captain received meat, fish, bows, arrows, clubs, targets (shields), and bear skins. Unwashed red and white bodies mingled amicably as attempts at communication were made. There was no common language between them, but by signs the Massawomecks indicated that they were returning from a raid on the people of the Sassafras River. They showed fresh wounds as evidence. They had been quite as startled as the discoverers at the unexpected encounter in mid-Bay.

When night fell the two groups separated, the Indians returning to the shore. Smith believed that they had agreed to meet again the next morning. But when the sun rose the anchored boat was alone and the beach was empty. The Massawomecks had disappeared. The discoverers never saw them again.

Smith thought that the Massawomecks came from well inland, and marks them on his map as being domiciled somewhere in the Maryland mountains, where for good measure he also puts in a stretch of shoreline to indicate the Western Ocean. However, their big canoes, and the trail of terror they had left among the tidewater tribes far down the Bay, suggests that they lived on one of the rivers connecting with the Bay. But, as with all the other native people who were indigenous to this region in the seventeenth century, all trace of them has by now long since disappeared, and we shall never know who they really were.

After this encounter, the expedition headed up the Sassafras River, which they called the Tockwough. Here they were again surrounded by heavily armed natives threatening them from canoes. These were of a different people using yet another language. But by luck one of them could speak the Powhatan tongue, and through this individual a parley was arranged. The crafty Captain showed them the arsenal of Massawomeck weapons he had on board and allowed them to believe that these had been taken forcibly from the departing raiding party. This was enough to make instant allies out of them.

Six or seven miles up the river, where the pretty yachting town of Georgetown, Maryland, now stands, the discoverers were welcomed into the Tockwough village. Here, "...their men, women and children, with dances, songs, fruits, fish, furres, and what they had, kindly intertained us, spreading mats for us to sit on, stretching their best abilities to express their loves...."

They noticed some unusual things about this village. Unlike all the others they had seen until now, it was surrounded by strong walls of logs and bark. It was a fortress in the wilderness, not unlike their own base at Jamestown. And, astonishingly, lying about were some knives and hatchets of European manufacture. The inhabitants said they had obtained these in trade from the Susquehannocks, "a mighty people, and mortal enemies of the Massawomecks," who lived several days journey above the Susquehanna falls. And where had the Susquehannocks got these implements? From the French in Canada, it transpired. By this time, French traders had already penetrated the St. Lawrence River and, that very summer of 1608, Samuel de Champlain was busy establishing his first settlement at Quebec, 700 miles to the north. The spread of these goods so rapidly to the upper Chesapeake region shows that the Iroquois-speaking people who dominated the northeastern part of the continent at this time had well-developed trade routes.

7. The Susquehannocks

"Such great and well proportioned men are seldome seen, for they seemed like Giants to the English, yea and to their neighbours; yet seemed of an honest and simple disposition."

John Smith, Description of Virginia, 1612.

   •   •   •

Captain Smith now resolved to meet the Susquehannocks. Since they lived beyond waters that could be reached by the discovery barge, he could not go to them. So, with his usual audacity, he decided that they must come to him.

Lengthy negotiations began with the interpreter from the Tockwough village who understood Powhatan. Another was found who spoke Susquehannock. Eventually these two embarked with the English and sailed to the first rapids on the Susquehanna River. The two Tockwoughs then departed upriver on foot, leaving Captain John and his men to wait.

THE SUSQUEHANNOCKS

For three or four days nothing happened. This enforced rest was a rare time of leisure for Captain and crew. They camped on the banks of this beautiful river, fished, gossiped, and mended their clothes.

The idyll ended abruptly with the appearance of some 60 huge Susquehannocks coming downriver in their canoes. The Tockwough intermediaries had done a good job, for the newcomers were friendly from the start. They brought presents of meat, tobacco, pipes, baskets, targets, and bows and arrows. The discoverers in turn presented small artifacts from the dwindling supply they had on the boat.

Unlike most encounters they had with the native peoples, this meeting seems to have been dominated by mutual admiration. Smith was greatly impressed by these people. Apparently they had loud voices, "... for their language it may well beseeme their proportions, sounding from them as it were a great voice in a vault, or cave, as an echo...." They wore clothes of skins, and in describing these the usually literate Smith gets himself into a rare tangle:

> ...some have Cassacks made of Beares heades and skinnes that a man's necks goes through the skinnes neck, and the eares of the beare fastened to his shoulders behind, the nose and teeth hanging downe his breast, and at the end of the nose hung a Beares paw; the half sleeves coming down to the elbows were the neckes of the Beares and the arms through the mouth, with pawes hanging at their noses....

The Susquehannock delegation was led by five chiefs, one of whom was larger than the rest and is described as having calves three-quarters of a yard around, ". . .and all the rest of his limbs so answerable to that proportion, that he seemed the goodliest man that ever we beheld." A picture of this person, almost certainly drawn by someone who had never seen an Indian, decorates a corner of Smith's 1612 *Map of Virginia*.

The gift-giving ceremonies completed, a hiatus developed which the English decided to fill by holding their habitual daily prayer meeting. They sang a psalm, "...at which solemnitie the poore Salvages much wondered."

Not to be outdone, the Susquehannocks returned the courtesy. "...they began in most passionate manner, to hold up their hands to the sunne, with a most fearful song. Then imbracing the Capitaine, they began to adore him in like manner...which don, with a most strange furious action and hellish voyce, began an oration of their loves." The celebration seems to have continued for some time, during which they showered the Captain with more gifts, all the while "stroking their ceremonious handes about his necke."

The use of tobacco in these ceremonies is interesting. It is curious that, anxious as he was to present the resources of Virginia in a favorable light, Smith does not even mention it in his various lists of useful commodities of the region. In the course of the next half century it would become the principal cash crop and source of wealth of the settlers. He had of course noted the Indians smoking it, and must have tried it himself during this and other meetings with them. Perhaps he did not like it, and could not imagine that his countrymen were about to start on a centuries-long addiction. Also, with his keen sense of where the political power lay, he may have wanted to avoid giving any offense to King James, who was well known as an anti-smoker. Some four years earlier the King had published his *Counterblaste to Tobacco* which made his position abundantly clear: "Smoking is a custome lothesome to the eye, hateful to the nose, harmful to the brain, dangerous to the lungs, and in the black and stinking fume therof nearest resembling the horrible Stygian smoke of the pit that is bottomless." The person who first recognized tobacco's commercial potential and introduced its systematic cultivation was John Rolfe, who became the husband of Pocahontas. Smith may have been the adventurer and discoverer, but it was Rolfe the innovator who provided the English in North America with their first economic base.

When the ceremonies of greeting were eventually concluded, it was decided that they would all go down the river and across the Bay to visit their mutual friends the Tockwoughs. But a strong wind had sprung up over the shoals at the river entrance, making it perilous for the fragile single-log river canoes to proceed. So, leaving men and canoes to follow later, the five chiefs boldly came aboard the English barge for the crossing. The distance is about 25 miles, which with luck they might have covered in five hours. The barge could have held few secrets from its passengers by the end of this trip: in particular, its aloneness and vulnerability must have been apparent. The chiefs, however, took no advantage of this insight.

Back at the Tockwough village, several days of ceremony and feasting ensued. This was in many ways the high point of the whole summer's exploration. Honored guests of intelligent and friendly natives, the visitors from Jamestown received homage, and became graciously and relaxedly drunk.

It gradually became clear that the Tockwough/Susquehannock alliance had a purpose in its hospitality. The two tribes were asking Captain Smith if he would lead them on a new campaign in their interminable and complicated war against the Massawomecks.

Smith would have dearly liked to do exactly that. This would not have been the first time that European explorers allied themselves with one Indian tribe to attack another: de Champlain was doing so that very moment in Canada. Also, Smith had few scruples about using force on the natives if it suited his purposes. On his return to London, he complained bitterly about the penurious attitude of the Council in Jamestown which had not allowed him enough boats, arms, and men to do a proper job of subjugating the tribes of the northern Bay. "But the councell then present, emulating [envying] his successe, would not thinke it fit to spare him 40. men to be hazarded in these unknowne regions...and so was lost that opportunitie." Much later, in 1622, he was still proposing to the Virginia Company that they send 100 soldiers and 30 sailors "...to inforce the Salvages to leave their country, or bring them in that feare and subjection that every man should follow their businesses securely." The Company replied, "...the charge [cost] would be too great." Smith's argument includes this revealing passage: "...besides, it is more easie to civilize them by conquest than faire means; for the one may be made at once, but their civilizing will require a long time and much industrie."

As it was, however, he knew that his small party was quite inadequate for such a task. So, promising to return again the following year (a promise he did not keep), he finally took leave of them and headed off into the Bay again, southwards towards home.

༺ ༺ ༺

8. The Righte Course How to Proceede

"…yet can wee not but lament that it was our ill fortune to end, when wee had but only learned how to begin, and found the right course how to proceede."

Richard Wiffin, William Phettiplace and Anas Todkill,
Proceedings of the English Colony of Virginia, 1612.

ಜಾ   ಜಾ   ಜಾ

The chronicle treats the return down the Bay, which took them close to three weeks, rather summarily, as if it were an anticlimax after their meetings with the Massawomecks and the Susquehannocks. Perhaps it was. However, this was the time when the exploration really got into its stride, when they filled in the gaps between the places they had already visited, when Captain John Smith took the notes and bearings which would enable him later, after returning to England, to draw his remarkably accurate map of the Bay country.

For the most part they kept to the western side of the Bay, investigating every major river they came to and leaving crosses carved on trees at the highest points they reached. They did make one venture over to the upper Eastern Shore and found a river which, confusingly, they identified as the Rappahannock. To judge from its position as shown on Smith's map, this Rappahannock was probably what is now called the Little Choptank. They did not go in behind the three large islands which lie parallel to the Eastern Shore: Kent Island (now the eastern landfall of the Chesapeake Bay Bridges), Poplar Island (then a single island much larger than it is today) and Sharp's Island (washed completely away during the early twentieth century and now marked only with a drunkenly-leaning light tower). Thus they missed three major rivers which would figure importantly in the later settlement of Maryland — the Chester, Miles, and Choptank Rivers.

They returned to Richard's Cliffs and explored the Patuxent. This river, they noted, "...is of lesser proportion than the rest: but the channell is 16. or 18. fadome deep in some places." It is today navigable for some 20 miles. They found the fish unusually plentiful here, and the people "most civill to give intertainment." Here, as elsewhere on the way down the Bay, the Captain earned favor and hospitality by promising that he would return the following year to beat up the Massawomecks. The summer of 1609 must have proved sorely disappointing to many gullible warriors of the Bay tribes.

When they reached Stingray Point, of painful memory, they went in for a second time to investigate the river now called the Rappahannock (they called it the Tappahannock, which is today the name of a pleasant market town some way up on its banks). Smith claimed it to be navigable for 130 miles: the actual distance on the modern chart is about 90 miles. The chroniclers, unaccountably, skip all details of their contacts with the peoples of that river, reporting only "...wee had much wrangling with that peevish nation; but, at last, they became as tractable as the rest."

As reported later by Smith in his *Generall Historie*, this was actually one of the most perilous confrontations of the whole voyage, one which came close to killing them all.

It started pleasantly enough. Close to the rivermouth they unexpectedly met up again with their old friend Mosco, the one with the beard who had helped them on the Potomac River. He tried to persuade them not to go on upriver into the territory of the Rappahannocks. Apparently the king of these people was angry at another nearby tribe which the English had recently befriended, because they had stolen three of his favorite women. The Indians operated on the principle that the friend of my enemy is also my enemy, and Mosco feared that the Rappahannocks would vent their wrath on Smith and his men.

The English dismissed this warning rather lightly. They were becoming overconfident, it seems. They thought that Mosco was simply trying to keep trade with these people in his own hands. So they continued, taking Mosco (who must have been a brave man) along with them.

After rowing a few miles up the river, they were greeted in the usual fashion by a small group of Indians standing on the shore, who beckoned them to come into a side creek. There, some canoes laden with produce, apparently as a gift for them, could be seen. They approached cautiously, and began to negotiate an exchange of hostages. Anas Todkill was this time the person chosen from the English side. He went ashore with the Indians, who appeared to be unarmed and few in number.

Then, however, he decided to take a walk over to the nearby woods. The Indians tried to prevent him, but suspicions aroused, he got far enough to see that there were many fighting men hidden in the trees. He shouted a warning to the men in the boat.

A nasty fracas ensued. Todkill was seized and held, while the braves in the woods loosed off a shower of arrows at the boat. The Indian hostage in the boat tried to jump overboard, but John Watkins, the soldier, pulled him back in and killed him on the spot. The English took shelter behind the Massawomeck shields they still had on board with them, and returned fire with their muskets.

Superior firepower eventually prevailed and the savages fled. Afterwards, more than a thousand spent arrows were counted on the ground. Miraculously, there were no serious injuries on the English side. Todkill, who had thrown himself flat on the ground when the first shots were fired, got back to the boat covered with Indian blood but otherwise unharmed. The Indians did not fare so well: "...we found some slaine, and in divers places much bloud."

Shaken by this incident, they used the rest of the day to rig the shields on sticks set in the gunwales along the sides of the barge, converting it into a veritable armored gunship. It was a wise precaution. Under way once more in the morning, they had gone only a short way when arrows flew again from the banks. What they thought to be clumps of small bushes materialized into the Rappahannock warriors once more. This time the arrows bounced off the shields and fell harmlessly into the water. They went on past, leaving their attackers "dauncing and singing very merrilie" (why they reacted thus is not explained).

Somewhere on this stretch of the Rappahannock one of their number, a Richard Featherstone, Gentleman, died of natural causes. He was an older man who had arrived in Jamestown with the first supply and had been with Smith on both voyages up the Bay. He had therefore spent almost all of his time since arriving in Virginia on the discovery barge. Smith thought highly of him, and wrote in eulogy: "...that all the time he had beene in this Country, had behaved himselfe honestly, valiantly, and industriously." They buried him in the night at a cove they called Featherstone Bay, and fired off a volley of shot over his grave. This place could be any one of dozens of attractive inlets off the main river which are now bordered with trim waterside homes. The bones of poor Richard Featherstone may still be resting there undisturbed beneath someone's well-tended lawn.

The people further up the river were known to Mosco and relatively friendly. Nevertheless, danger was not over. Sailing on "so high as our boat would float," they were busy engraving the usual cross and their names on some trees when a single arrow came winging out of nowhere. They searched around for an hour, "not seeing well where a Salvage could hide himselfe," then suddenly were attacked by a hundred of them who must have been there all along. Mosco must have been feeling particularly belligerent that day, for he shot off all his arrows, rushed back to the boat for more, and then, when the attackers took off, chased them until they were almost out of sight. Returning, he found a savage who had been wounded in the knee lying on the ground, and attacked him viciously. "Never was a Dog more furious against a Beare, than Mosco was to have beat out his braines." The English hauled him off and pacified him by gathering up and giving to him all the spent arrows they could find (arrows were a recyclable weapon for the Indians), while Surgeon Bagnall attended to the injured man's wounds.

Then, through Mosco, they interviewed this man. Smith asked why the Indians had attacked without provocation, and the man replied, prophetically, that he had heard the white men were "...a people come from under the world to take their world from them." He believed that the English were actually dead people temporarily returned to earth (Columbus encountered the same belief among the natives of the Caribbean); but he admitted that he knew no more worlds than those under the sky which covered him. He explained that there were four separate hunting parties from his people ranging in the area, and he invited the discoverers to meet with them the following day. Smith decided to take him along.

They started back downriver after nightfall, which they hoped would lessen the risk of ambush from the high banks which line the river on both sides in this area. They had not gone far before another shower of arrows announced the presence of more Indians. They made it to an open bay where they anchored for the night. When morning came, it turned out that these were the people of their prisoner. More parlaying took place, during which the man was understood to have explained to his chiefs on the shore that it was impossible to hurt these beings, who had supernatural powers, so they might as well be friends. They took his advice, and feasting and gift-giving followed. These simple hunter-gatherers had not realized what the Englishmen's pistols were for, and asked for some to use as tobacco pipes. They had to be satisfied with other gifts.

The boat still had to pass through the territory of the Rappahannocks again before reaching the open Bay. This time Smith, confident of support from the tribes upriver, approached them brusquely. By messenger (probably Mosco) he let it be known that he was displeased to have been attacked twice on the way up — he that came "onely in love, to do them good" — and therefore he would "burne all their houses, destroy their corne, and for ever hold them enemies, till they made him satisfaction."

A response came back: "what satisfaction?" Smith proposed, among other things, that the Rappahannock king's son be delivered as a hostage. This proved too much for the king (his son was an only one), but he came up with an ingenious counterproposal: he would give Smith the three women who had been stolen from him earlier, if he (Smith) could arrange for their recovery. Smith accepted.

The concluding scene of this drama took place in the village of the womens' abductors, with its chief, the Rappahannock chief, and Captain Smith, each with their entourages of supporters, in attendance. The three women were brought out, and Smith gave each of them a chain of beads. They hoped they were coming with him. But the Captain, who knew a thing or two, had earlier decided that their presence in the boat and at Jamestown would not exactly promote peace and harmony among his men. So, after accepting them as gifts in the proper manner, he turned and presented them back. He offered first choice to Chief Rappahannock, bidding him to "take her he loved best." The next choice went to the chief of the kidnappers. The woman who remained was presented to Mosco. This masterly piece of diplomacy accomplished, they fell to feasting and singing again, promising ever to be friends. The English barge then departed, firing a volley in farewell salute.

Out on the Bay and underway again, they pressed on southward without stopping. Approaching Old Point Comfort, at the mouth of the James River, after dark in a flat calm, they were hit by a typical heat-induced thunderstorm and had to bail furiously to remain afloat. The description of this storm in the chronicle reminds us that these men used the language of Shakespeare and the King James version of the Bible "...yet running before the winde, at last we made land by the flashes of fire from heaven, by which light only we kept from the splitting shore, until it pleased God in that black darkness, to preserve us by that light to find Point Comfort."

They ventured briefly up one more unexplored river on the south side of the James entrance, probably passing where the Port of Norfolk is now located. Here they met with more Indians, more arrows, more treachery followed by reconciliation—a routine sequence by now.

Finally, they made it up the river to Jamestown, where they arrived on September 7, 1608, 45 days after their second departure from there. They found "M. Scrivener and divers others well recovered, many dead, some sicke; the late President (Ratcliffe) prisoner for muteny...."

In other words, little had changed while they were away.

9. The Memory of Time

"History is the memory of time, the life of the dead, the happiness of the living."

John Smith, *Generall Historie*, 1624.

"Here lies one conquer'd that hath conquer'd Kings:
Subdu'd large Territories, and done things
Which to the World impossible would seeme,
But that the truth is held in more esteeme."

John Smith's Epitaph, 1631.
(written by himself shortly before his death)

ප ප ප

The discovery of the Chesapeake was in fact the principal accomplishment of the colony's second summer, that of the year 1608, since little else was achieved. A harvest of sorts was gathered, but it was badly stored by the improvident settlers and most was destroyed by rain or rats. These were, incidentally, English ship's rats, whose colony was prospering mightily. Captain Smith, who was formally sworn in as President a few days after his return, had to turn immediately to the business of securing from Powhatan's indians a supply of corn sufficient to see them through the winter. He had no more time for explorations.

During the next 12 months he was fully occupied with trying to manage this increasingly ungovernable little community. He pulled them through, but in doing so made more and more enemies, so that the politics of the place became ever more polarized between those who supported Smith and those who hated him.

In September, 1609, he was returning by boat from a trip to the head of the James River, where he had been trying to placate some mutineers who had established a separate settlement, when a powder keg lying on the floorboards at his feet exploded, setting him on fire and seriously injuring his legs. He jumped overboard to put out the flames and nearly drowned before his companions could haul him back.

He was in poor condition when they got him back to Jamestown. The colonists, some with undisguised satisfaction, wrote him off for dead. When, after some days, it seemed that he might live after all, one of them came to his bedside in the night and tried to murder him with a pistol, which fortunately misfired. They should have known better: the indestructable Smith would survive for more than 20 years yet. But, temporarily crippled, and, one suspects, profoundly discouraged by the deteriorating political situation in Jamestown, he relinquished the Presidency and took the next boat home to England. He never saw the Chesapeake country again.

One flower of his summer of discoveries on the Bay was his remarkably accurate *Map of Virginia* which was published in Oxford in 1612.

Not everyone admired what he had done. Many charged these explorations had been a waste of time because nothing valuable had been found. Why, it was frequently asked, had they failed to discover gold and silver, spoil and pillage, like the much-envied Spanish further south? In a piece written by three of Smith's faithful supporters, one of whom was Anas Todkill, there is this spirited and poetic defense:

But we chanced in a lande even as God made it. Where we found only an idle, improvident, scattered peoples, ignorant of the knowledge of gold, or silver, or any commodities; and carelesse of any thing but from hand to mouth, but for baubles of no worth; nothing to encourage us but what accidently wee found nature afforded... and tell mee how many ever, with such small meanes as a barge of 2. Tunnes, sometimes with 7. 8. 9. or but at most 15 men, did ever discover so many faire and navigable rivers, subject so many severall kings people and nations to obedience and contribution, with so little bloud shed....

The rest of Smith's life was energetic and fruitful, but marked with the kind of gathering indignation which so often befalls men of action who are removed prematurely from the game. He never did understand quite why he was shunted aside.

He applied several times to go back to Virginia in one capacity or another, but he had too many enemies there and in London to be accepted. Furthermore, he was not quite a gentleman, and this began to be an increasingly important consideration as realization of the potential of the struggling colony spread. For several years he was active in Virginia Company affairs in London, acting as a sort of pundit on conditions in the colony and spending much time indignantly defending his record and vilifying his critics.

During these years, he was able to hammer at an unassailable point: that things had not gone well in Jamestown since his departure. During the dreadful winter of 1609-10, the settlement was reduced from about 500 to 60 souls by starvation, accidents, and Indian harassment. Some of the settlers had even boiled and eaten an Indian. One man killed his wife (women had begun to arrive from England by this time) and salted her down for later consumption. When discovered, he was burned at the stake (the English could be savages, too). Following the astonishing arrival in May 1610 of the passengers and crew of the missing *Sea Venture*, which had been wrecked on Bermuda (they came in two homemade boats built on the beach there from wreckage), the colony was actually abandoned and evacuation commenced. The survivors were part way down the James River on their way to England when, by another almost incredible coincidence, they met a ship on her way up, coming directly from England and bearing Lord Delaware, their new Governor. He ordered them back, and the colony survived, but only just.

In London in 1616, John Smith met with Pocahontas once again. While they were still in Virginia she had tried, as was her duty under Indian custom, to convert him to her ways; but, as would so often happen during the first collisions between Europeans and the primitive peoples of new lands, she wound up being converted to his. Some years after Smith left Virginia, she, believing him to be dead, had allowed herself to be declared a Christian and married to the worthy but dull John Rolfe. They had a son, Thomas Rolfe, whom the many people who claim to be descended from Pocahontas must necessarily count as their ancestor also. She and the baby Thomas went with Rolfe to England, where she became an instant celebrity in London society and a favorite of Queen Anne. When she heard that John Smith was there, alive and well, she became very upset and, after meeting with him, refused to talk to anyone for days. Less than a year after her arrival in England, at about age 20, she fell ill from a respiratory infection. She died while onboard the ship which was to carry her back to Virginia, and was buried at Gravesend, on the River Thames.

Her father, Powhatan, continued his policy of tolerating the English settlement in his territory for some time after Smith's tenure as president. It would cost him and his people dearly. In an earlier conversation with Powhatan, Smith recorded the Indian leader as stating "...for many doe informe, your coming here is not for trade, but to invade my people and posesse my Countrie." Smith of course denied it, but the old chief had hit the nail on the head. As more and more Englishmen and, very significantly, the first Englishwomen arrived, it became ever plainer to him that these were not temporary visitors in the nature of a migrant hunting party of his own people. Furthermore, he received some thought-provoking intelligence about the English upon the return of a worthy elder of the tribe called Tomocomo whom he had sent to London with Pocahontas. This gentleman had been instructed to carry a stick with him and secretly put a notch on it for each fighting man he saw. Wisely, he gave up counting after a short while. Tomocomo found it hard to believe that the sickly and effeminate King James really was the highest ruler of this great and powerful tribe, and was much offended that they would not take him to meet God.

Powhatan eventually moved his camp further inland, where he died in 1618. A successor Powhatan (the name was a titular one) tried a concerted attack on the English in 1622, but by then it was far too late. They had already possessed his country.

Smith himself eventually transferred his attentions to New England, and voyaged there in 1613 and again in 1615, producing another superb map and collecting for himself the resounding title "Admirall of New England," but no further gainful employment. When he heard that the *Mayflower* was preparing to carry yet another group of settlers to the New World, he applied for the job of Captain of that expedition (a position akin to Chief of Security in modern parlance). The Pilgrims, advised of his prickly character, chose instead Miles Standish, who gained a place among history's immortals for his bashful and unsuccessful courtship-by-proxy of Priscilla Mullins. One has the feeling that, had our Captain got the job, Mistress Mullins would have been wooed in a more forthright fashion.

In his later years, Smith turned increasingly to writing. He produced, among other things, the *Generall Historie of Virginia, New England and the Summer Isles* (1624), an ambitious but hastily-written work describing the English settlement of the entire American eastern coast and Bermuda. He also published a very curious work, the *Accidence for Young Seamen* (1627), which was the first manual in English of the mariner's trade.

He never married or had a permanent home. He moved about constantly, staying with acquaintances, of whom he had many, although few if any appear to have been truly his friends.

He died in London in 1631, aged 51, at the house of one such acquaintance. He was buried in a church which was subsequently destroyed in the Great Fire, so that his resting place there perished also. One of the few memorials to be erected in his honor anywhere is a plaque in the Capitol building in Washington, D.C., close to the Potomac River and the Bay which he discovered nearly four centuries earlier. There is also a statue of him at the site of Jamestown (now a National Park) where he poses heriocally, gazing out over the James

56   *DISCOVERY OF THE CHESAPEAKE*

River, his back turned on the nearby smaller statue of Pocahontas.

One has the feeling that he would have cared little for these material tributes. It is probably through books about him, like this one, that he would really wish to be remembered.

A Note on Sources

The main contemporary record of Captain Smith's voyages of discovery on the Bay is contained in two chapters of *The Proceedings of the English Colony in Virginia,* co-authored by Walter Russel (the doctor), Anas Todkill, and various other participants in the two expeditions. The *Proceedings* were first published in Oxford in 1612 as an annex to Smith's own *Map of Virginia (With a description of the Countrey, the Commodities, People, Government, and Religeon, Written by Capitaine Smith, Sometime Gouvernour of the Countrey).* The latter work is based in large part on Smith's observations during the 1608 voyages of exploration, and mentions explicitly many of the incidents that occurred.

If the Captain ever kept a personal log of the trip it has never been found. This omission allowed the modern writer John Barth to base his comic novel, *The Sot-weed Factor,* on the supposed discovery of a secret diary in which the Captain tells all.

The account in the *Proceedings*, revised extensively in places by Smith, but still attributed to the same authors, reappears in Smith's *Generall Historie of Virginia, New England and the Summer Isles,* published in 1624.

Smith's other writings, which were prolific, are well documented elsewhere, notably in a massive annotated compendium, *The Complete Works of Captain John Smith*, published by Arber in Edinburgh during the late nineteenth century.

There are several other contemporary accounts of the first years at Jamestown written by people who were there, but most of them were not admirers of the Captain and make little reference to his exploratory achievements. Smith's own account of the first year there, entitled *A True Relation (of such occurrences and Accidents of Note as hath Happened in Virginia since the First Planting of that Collony),* was published in London in 1608, while Smith was still in Virginia. It therefore tells the story only up to the point where this one begins, with the departure of the *Phenix,* which must have carried his handwritten draft with it.

Subsequent re-examinations of the events of the period have been plentiful, although as mentioned earlier most of them treat the 1608 voyages of discovery rather summarily. This writer's references included John Fisk's magisterial history, *Old Virginia and her Neighbours* (1897), Katherine Wood's *The True Story of Captain Smith* (1901), and Philip Barbour's *The Three Worlds of Captain Smith* (1963). Another modern retelling of the story is *Pocahontas*, by Frances Mossiker (1976), which is doubly interesting because it tries to interpret what happened from the Indians' side and from a woman's point of view.

Mention must also be made of the positive avalanche of poetry and prose which appeared in late Victorian times, and has recurred at intervals since, as romantic authors have rediscovered what they interpret as one of history's great love affairs between Pocahontas and an idealized, sanitized John Smith. Many modern school history books still seem to be based on this copious body of sentimental and inaccurate blather.

Finally, for details of other incidents in the early history of colonization in America, I have consulted mainly Samuel Eliot Morison's *The European Discovery of North America*.

APPENDIX

The Crews of the Discovery Barge

First Voyage
John Smith .... Captain
Walter Russel .... Doctor
Ralph Morton .... Gentleman
Thomas Momford .... Gentleman
William Cantrill .... Gentleman
Richard Featherstone .... Gentleman
James Bourne .... Gentleman
Michael Sicklemore .... Gentleman
Anas Todkill .... Soldier
Robert Small .... Soldier
James Watkins .... Soldier
John Powell .... Soldier
James Read .... Blacksmith
Richard Keale .... Fishmonger
Jonas Profit .... Fisherman

Second Voyage
John Smith .... Captain
Nathaniel Powell .... Gentleman
Thomas Momford .... Gentleman
Richard Featherstone .... Gentleman
Michael Sicklemore .... Gentleman
James Bourne .... Gentleman
Anas Todkill .... Soldier
Edward Pysing .... Soldier
Richard Keale .... Soldier
Anthony Bagnall .... Soldier
James Watkins .... Soldier
William Ward .... Tailor
Jonas Profit .... Fisherman

About the Author

Francis d'A. Collings was born in England in 1929, studied economics in Canada and the United States, and worked with the International Monetary Fund in Washington, D. C., from 1959 to 1985. He has sailed the Chesapeake Bay for many years, and after retirement put this experience to work in the compiling of this book. He now resides on the island of Guernsey in the English Channel Islands.

About the Illustrator

Leonard Vosburgh was born in Yonkers, N. Y., in 1912. He worked as a lithographer before attending Pratt Institute of Art in New York. After graduation, he worked as an advertising artist for several years, then decided to become a book illustrator. In 1970, Mr. Vosburgh also became a regional artist, doing watercolors of the Eastern Shore for the period 1868-1930. He and his wife, Alberta, spend summers on their boat at Oxford, Maryland. *Discovery of the Chesapeake* is the 91st book he has illustrated.

Other publications of the Chesapeake Bay Maritime Museum:

Chesapeake Bay Sloops
      by Thomas C. Gillmer, N.A.

Chesapeake Bay Crabbing Skiffs
      by Howard I. Chapelle

The Edna E. Lockwood (a Chesapeake Bay bugeye)
      by Charles H. Kepner

Notes on Chesapeake Bay Skipjacks
      by Howard I. Chapelle

Captain John Smith's Map of Virginia, reproduced from an engraving in the Library of Congress.